60 Days Away Journal

NAME ________________________

ADDRESS ________________________

PHONE ________________________

E-MAIL ________________________

Welcome to Your 60-Day Gratitude & Highlights Journal!

This journal is your personal space to slow down, reflect, and appreciate the moments that make life meaningful. Over the next 60 days, you'll have the opportunity to cultivate a habit of gratitude, celebrate your daily highlights, and shift your focus toward the positive.

Each day, take a few minutes to acknowledge what you're grateful for, set an intention for the day, and capture the moments that brought you joy or growth. There are no strict rules—just an open space for you to express yourself, gain clarity, and embrace life's simple yet powerful moments.

Enjoy this journey of self-reflection and appreciation, and watch how small moments of gratitude can create lasting happiness

ABOUT ME

Date: /   /

Name:

Why I started journaling:

My Goals

My Motivations

Reason 1:

Reason 2:

Reason 3:

My Habit

New Healthy Habits

Bad Habits To Reduce

Rewards

Rewards For Meeting My Goals

Why I Deserve These

1.

2.

3.

4.

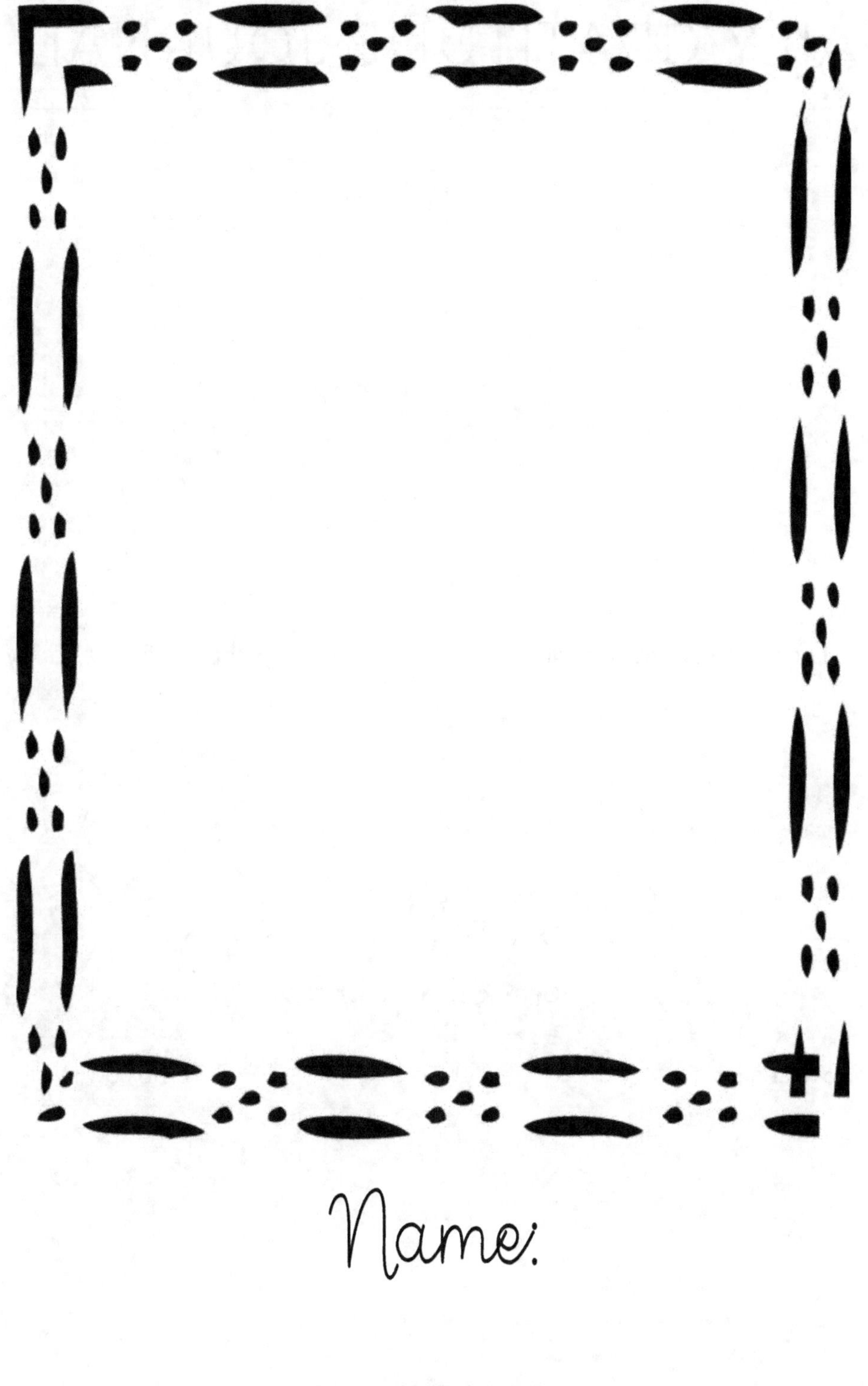
Name:

DAILY GRATITUDE JOURNAL

Date: /   /

Today I am grateful for

Quotes & Affirmations

Looking Forward To Today

Things that make me happy

Getting Better Each Day

My Challenge

Let Go Of

Tomorrow I Will

HIGHLIGHTS

Date: /   /

Highlights of the Day

1.

2.

3.

What is something new you've learned?

What were some challenges you faced?

What is the best thing you have done for yourself today?

Has practicing gratitude helped you today?

YES   MAYBE   NO

DAILY GRATITUDE JOURNAL

Date: /   /

Today I am grateful for

Quotes & Affirmations

Looking Forward To Today

Things that make me happy

Getting Better Each Day

My Challenge

Let Go Of

Tomorrow I Will

HIGHLIGHTS

Date: /   /

Highlights of the Day

1.

2.

3.

What is something new you've learned?

What were some challenges you faced?

What is the best thing you have done for yourself today?

Has practicing gratitude helped you today?

YES   MAYBE   NO

DAILY GRATITUDE JOURNAL

Date: /   /

Today I am grateful for

Quotes & Affirmations

Looking Forward To Today

Things that make me happy

Getting Better Each Day

My Challenge

Let Go Of

Tomorrow I Will

HIGHLIGHTS

Date: /   /

Highlights of the Day

1.

2.

3.

What is something new you've learned?

What were some challenges you faced?

What is the best thing you have done for yourself today?

Has practicing gratitude helped you today?

YES   MAYBE   NO

DAILY GRATITUDE JOURNAL

Date: /   /

Today I am grateful for

Quotes & Affirmations

Looking Forward To Today

Things that make me happy

Getting Better Each Day

My Challenge

Let Go Of

Tomorrow I Will

HIGHLIGHTS

Date: /   /

Highlights of the Day

1.

2.

3.

What is something new you've learned?

What were some challenges you faced?

What is the best thing you have done for yourself today?

Has practicing gratitude helped you today?

YES   MAYBE   NO

DAILY GRATITUDE JOURNAL

Date: /   /

Today I am grateful for

Quotes & Affirmations

Looking Forward To Today

Things that make me happy

Getting Better Each Day

My Challenge

Let Go Of

Tomorrow I Will

HIGHLIGHTS

Date: /   /

Highlights of the Day

1.

2.

3.

What is something new you've learned?

What were some challenges you faced?

What is the best thing you have done for yourself today?

Has practicing gratitude helped you today?

YES   MAYBE   NO

DAILY GRATITUDE JOURNAL

Date: /   /

Today I am grateful for

Quotes & Affirmations

Looking Forward To Today

Things that make me happy

Getting Better Each Day

My Challenge

Let Go Of

Tomorrow I Will

HIGHLIGHTS

Date: /   /

Highlights of the Day

1.

2.

3.

What is something new you've learned?

What were some challenges you faced?

What is the best thing you have done for yourself today?

Has practicing gratitude helped you today?

YES   MAYBE   NO

DAILY GRATITUDE JOURNAL

Date: /   /

Today I am grateful for

Quotes & Affirmations

Looking Forward To Today

Things that make me happy

Getting Better Each Day

My Challenge

Let Go Of

Tomorrow I Will

HIGHLIGHTS

Date: /   /

Highlights of the Day

1.

2.

3.

What is something new you've learned?

What were some challenges you faced?

What is the best thing you have done for yourself today?

Has practicing gratitude helped you today?

YES　　　　MAYBE　　　　NO

DAILY GRATITUDE JOURNAL

Date: / /

Today I am grateful for

Quotes & Affirmations

Looking Forward To Today

Things that make me happy

Getting Better Each Day

My Challenge	Let Go Of	Tomorrow I Will

HIGHLIGHTS

Date: /   /

Highlights of the Day

1.

2.

3.

What is something new you've learned?

What were some challenges you faced?

What is the best thing you have done for yourself today?

Has practicing gratitude helped you today?

YES   MAYBE   NO

DAILY GRATITUDE JOURNAL

Date: /   /

Today I am grateful for

Quotes & Affirmations

Looking Forward To Today

Things that make me happy

Getting Better Each Day

My Challenge

Let Go Of

Tomorrow I Will

HIGHLIGHTS

Date: /   /

Highlights of the Day

1.

2.

3.

What is something new you've learned?

What were some challenges you faced?

What is the best thing you have done for yourself today?

Has practicing gratitude helped you today?

YES   MAYBE   NO

DAILY GRATITUDE JOURNAL

Date: /   /

Today I am grateful for

Quotes & Affirmations

Looking Forward To Today

Things that make me happy

Getting Better Each Day

My Challenge

Let Go Of

Tomorrow I Will

HIGHLIGHTS

Date: /   /

Highlights of the Day

1.

2.

3.

What is something new you've learned?

What were some challenges you faced?

What is the best thing you have done for yourself today?

Has practicing gratitude helped you today?

YES   MAYBE   NO

DAILY GRATITUDE JOURNAL

Date: / /

Today I am grateful for

Quotes & Affirmations

Looking Forward To Today

Things that make me happy

Getting Better Each Day

My Challenge

Let Go Of

Tomorrow I Will

HIGHLIGHTS

Date: /   /

Highlights of the Day

1.

2.

3.

What is something new you've learned?

What were some challenges you faced?

What is the best thing you have done for yourself today?

Has practicing gratitude helped you today?

YES   MAYBE   NO

DAILY GRATITUDE JOURNAL

Date: /   /

Today I am grateful for

Quotes & Affirmations

Looking Forward To Today

Things that make me happy

Getting Better Each Day

My Challenge

Let Go Of

Tomorrow I Will

HIGHLIGHTS

Date: / /

Highlights of the Day

1.

2.

3.

What is something new you've learned?

What were some challenges you faced?

What is the best thing you have done for yourself today?

Has practicing gratitude helped you today?

YES   MAYBE   NO

DAILY GRATITUDE JOURNAL

Date: /   /

Today I am grateful for

Quotes & Affirmations

Looking Forward To Today

Things that make me happy

Getting Better Each Day

My Challenge

Let Go Of

Tomorrow I Will

HIGHLIGHTS

Date: /   /

Highlights of the Day

1.

2.

3.

What is something new you've learned?

What were some challenges you faced?

What is the best thing you have done for yourself today?

Has practicing gratitude helped you today?

YES	MAYBE	NO

DAILY GRATITUDE JOURNAL

Date: /   /

Today I am grateful for

Quotes & Affirmations

Looking Forward To Today

Things that make me happy

Getting Better Each Day

My Challenge

Let Go Of

Tomorrow I Will

HIGHLIGHTS

Date: /   /

Highlights of the Day

1.

2.

3.

What is something new you've learned?

What were some challenges you faced?

What is the best thing you have done for yourself today?

Has practicing gratitude helped you today?

YES   MAYBE   NO

DAILY GRATITUDE JOURNAL

Date: /   /

Today I am grateful for

Quotes & Affirmations

Looking Forward To Today

Things that make me happy

Getting Better Each Day

My Challenge

Let Go Of

Tomorrow I Will

HIGHLIGHTS

Date: /   /

Highlights of the Day

1.

2.

3.

What is something new you've learned?

What were some challenges you faced?

What is the best thing you have done for yourself today?

Has practicing gratitude helped you today?

YES   MAYBE   NO

DAILY GRATITUDE JOURNAL

Date: /   /

Today I am grateful for

Quotes & Affirmations

Looking Forward To Today

Things that make me happy

Getting Better Each Day

My Challenge

Let Go Of

Tomorrow I Will

HIGHLIGHTS

Date: / /

Highlights of the Day

1.

2.

3.

What is something new you've learned?

What were some challenges you faced?

What is the best thing you have done for yourself today?

Has practicing gratitude helped you today?

YES   MAYBE   NO

DAILY GRATITUDE JOURNAL

Date: ___ / ___ / ___

Today I am grateful for

Quotes & Affirmations

Looking Forward To Today

Things that make me happy

Getting Better Each Day

My Challenge

Let Go Of

Tomorrow I Will

HIGHLIGHTS

Date: /   /

Highlights of the Day

1.

2.

3.

What is something new you've learned?

What were some challenges you faced?

What is the best thing you have done for yourself today?

Has practicing gratitude helped you today?

YES   MAYBE   NO

DAILY GRATITUDE JOURNAL

Date: /   /

Today I am grateful for

Quotes & Affirmations

Looking Forward To Today

Things that make me happy

Getting Better Each Day

My Challenge	Let Go Of	Tomorrow I Will

HIGHLIGHTS

Date: /   /

Highlights of the Day

1.

2.

3.

What is something new you've learned?

What were some challenges you faced?

What is the best thing you have done for yourself today?

Has practicing gratitude helped you today?

YES   MAYBE   NO

DAILY GRATITUDE JOURNAL

Date: / /

Today I am grateful for

Quotes & Affirmations

Looking Forward To Today

Things that make me happy

Getting Better Each Day

My Challenge

Let Go Of

Tomorrow I Will

HIGHLIGHTS

Date: / /

Highlights of the Day

1.

2.

3.

What is something new you've learned?

What were some challenges you faced?

What is the best thing you have done for yourself today?

Has practicing gratitude helped you today?

YES   MAYBE   NO

DAILY GRATITUDE JOURNAL

Date: /   /

Today I am grateful for

Quotes & Affirmations

Looking Forward To Today

Things that make me happy

Getting Better Each Day

My Challenge	Let Go Of	Tomorrow I Will

HIGHLIGHTS

Date: /   /

Highlights of the Day

1.

2.

3.

What is something new you've learned?

What were some challenges you faced?

What is the best thing you have done for yourself today?

Has practicing gratitude helped you today?

YES   MAYBE   NO

DAILY GRATITUDE JOURNAL

Date: /   /

Today I am grateful for

Quotes & Affirmations

Looking Forward To Today

Things that make me happy

Getting Better Each Day

My Challenge

Let Go Of

Tomorrow I Will

HIGHLIGHTS

Date: /   /

Highlights of the Day

1.

2.

3.

What is something new you've learned?

What were some challenges you faced?

What is the best thing you have done for yourself today?

Has practicing gratitude helped you today?

YES   MAYBE   NO

DAILY GRATITUDE JOURNAL

Date: /   /

Today I am grateful for

Quotes & Affirmations

Looking Forward To Today

Things that make me happy

Getting Better Each Day

My Challenge

Let Go Of

Tomorrow I Will

HIGHLIGHTS

Date: /   /

Highlights of the Day

1.

2.

3.

What is something new you've learned?

What were some challenges you faced?

What is the best thing you have done for yourself today?

Has practicing gratitude helped you today?

YES   MAYBE   NO

DAILY GRATITUDE JOURNAL

Date: /   /

Today I am grateful for

Quotes & Affirmations

Looking Forward To Today

Things that make me happy

Getting Better Each Day

My Challenge

Let Go Of

Tomorrow I Will

HIGHLIGHTS

Date: /   /

Highlights of the Day

1.

2.

3.

What is something new you've learned?

What were some challenges you faced?

What is the best thing you have done for yourself today?

Has practicing gratitude helped you today?

YES   MAYBE   NO

DAILY GRATITUDE JOURNAL

Date: /   /

Today I am grateful for

Quotes & Affirmations

Looking Forward To Today

Things that make me happy

Getting Better Each Day

My Challenge

Let Go Of

Tomorrow I Will

HIGHLIGHTS

Date: / /

Highlights of the Day

1.

2.

3.

What is something new you've learned?

What were some challenges you faced?

What is the best thing you have done for yourself today?

Has practicing gratitude helped you today?

YES	MAYBE	NO

DAILY GRATITUDE JOURNAL

Date: /   /

Today I am grateful for

Quotes & Affirmations

Looking Forward To Today

Things that make me happy

Getting Better Each Day

My Challenge

Let Go Of

Tomorrow I Will

HIGHLIGHTS

Date: /   /

Highlights of the Day

1.

2.

3.

What is something new you've learned?

What were some challenges you faced?

What is the best thing you have done for yourself today?

Has practicing gratitude helped you today?

YES   MAYBE   NO

DAILY GRATITUDE JOURNAL

Date: /   /

Today I am grateful for

Quotes & Affirmations

Looking Forward To Today

Things that make me happy

Getting Better Each Day

My Challenge

Let Go Of

Tomorrow I Will

HIGHLIGHTS

Date: /   /

Highlights of the Day

1.

2.

3.

What is something new you've learned?

What were some challenges you faced?

What is the best thing you have done for yourself today?

Has practicing gratitude helped you today?

YES   MAYBE   NO

DAILY GRATITUDE JOURNAL

Date: /   /

Today I am grateful for

Quotes & Affirmations

Looking Forward To Today

Things that make me happy

Getting Better Each Day

My Challenge

Let Go Of

Tomorrow I Will

HIGHLIGHTS

Date: /   /

Highlights of the Day

1.

2.

3.

What is something new you've learned?

What were some challenges you faced?

What is the best thing you have done for yourself today?

Has practicing gratitude helped you today?

YES   MAYBE   NO

DAILY GRATITUDE JOURNAL

Date: / /

Today I am grateful for

Quotes & Affirmations

Looking Forward To Today

Things that make me happy

Getting Better Each Day

My Challenge

Let Go Of

Tomorrow I Will

HIGHLIGHTS

Date: /   /

Highlights of the Day

1.

2.

3.

What is something new you've learned?

What were some challenges you faced?

What is the best thing you have done for yourself today?

Has practicing gratitude helped you today?

YES   MAYBE   NO

DAILY GRATITUDE JOURNAL

Date: /   /

Today I am grateful for

Quotes & Affirmations

Looking Forward To Today

Things that make me happy

Getting Better Each Day

My Challenge

Let Go Of

Tomorrow I Will

HIGHLIGHTS

Date: /   /

Highlights of the Day

1.

2.

3.

What is something new you've learned?

What were some challenges you faced?

What is the best thing you have done for yourself today?

Has practicing gratitude helped you today?

YES	MAYBE	NO

DAILY GRATITUDE JOURNAL

Date: /   /

Today I am grateful for

Quotes & Affirmations

Looking Forward To Today

Things that make me happy

Getting Better Each Day

My Challenge

Let Go Of

Tomorrow I Will

HIGHLIGHTS

Date: /   /

Highlights of the Day

1.

2.

3.

What is something new you've learned?

What were some challenges you faced?

What is the best thing you have done for yourself today?

Has practicing gratitude helped you today?

YES   MAYBE   NO

DAILY GRATITUDE JOURNAL

Date: /   /

Today I am grateful for

Quotes & Affirmations

Looking Forward To Today

Things that make me happy

Getting Better Each Day

My Challenge

Let Go Of

Tomorrow I Will

HIGHLIGHTS

Date: /   /

Highlights of the Day

1.

2.

3.

What is something new you've learned?

What were some challenges you faced?

What is the best thing you have done for yourself today?

Has practicing gratitude helped you today?

YES   MAYBE   NO

DAILY GRATITUDE JOURNAL

Date: /   /

Today I am grateful for

Quotes & Affirmations

Looking Forward To Today

Things that make me happy

Getting Better Each Day

My Challenge

Let Go Of

Tomorrow I Will

HIGHLIGHTS

Date: /   /

Highlights of the Day

1.

2.

3.

What is something new you've learned?

What were some challenges you faced?

What is the best thing you have done for yourself today?

Has practicing gratitude helped you today?

YES   MAYBE   NO

DAILY GRATITUDE JOURNAL

Date: / /

Today I am grateful for

Quotes & Affirmations

Looking Forward To Today

Things that make me happy

Getting Better Each Day

My Challenge

Let Go Of

Tomorrow I Will

HIGHLIGHTS

Date: /   /

Highlights of the Day

1.

2.

3.

What is something new you've learned?

What were some challenges you faced?

What is the best thing you have done for yourself today?

Has practicing gratitude helped you today?

YES   MAYBE   NO

DAILY GRATITUDE JOURNAL

Date: /   /

Today I am grateful for

Quotes & Affirmations

Looking Forward To Today

Things that make me happy

Getting Better Each Day

My Challenge

Let Go Of

Tomorrow I Will

HIGHLIGHTS

Date: /   /

Highlights of the Day

1.

2.

3.

What is something new you've learned?

What were some challenges you faced?

What is the best thing you have done for yourself today?

Has practicing gratitude helped you today?

YES	MAYBE	NO

DAILY GRATITUDE JOURNAL

Date: /   /

Today I am grateful for

Quotes & Affirmations

Looking Forward To Today

Things that make me happy

Getting Better Each Day

My Challenge

Let Go Of

Tomorrow I Will

HIGHLIGHTS

Date: /   /

Highlights of the Day

1.

2.

3.

What is something new you've learned?

What were some challenges you faced?

What is the best thing you have done for yourself today?

Has practicing gratitude helped you today?

YES   MAYBE   NO

DAILY GRATITUDE JOURNAL

Date: /   /

Today I am grateful for

Quotes & Affirmations

Looking Forward To Today

Things that make me happy

Getting Better Each Day

My Challenge

Let Go Of

Tomorrow I Will

HIGHLIGHTS

Date: /   /

Highlights of the Day

1.

2.

3.

What is something new you've learned?

What were some challenges you faced?

What is the best thing you have done for yourself today?

Has practicing gratitude helped you today?

YES   MAYBE   NO

DAILY GRATITUDE JOURNAL

Date: /   /

Today I am grateful for

Quotes & Affirmations

Looking Forward To Today

Things that make me happy

Getting Better Each Day

My Challenge

Let Go Of

Tomorrow I Will

HIGHLIGHTS

Date: /   /

Highlights of the Day

1.

2.

3.

What is something new you've learned?

What were some challenges you faced?

What is the best thing you have done for yourself today?

Has practicing gratitude helped you today?

YES   MAYBE   NO

DAILY GRATITUDE JOURNAL

Date: / /

Today I am grateful for

Quotes & Affirmations

Looking Forward To Today

Things that make me happy

Getting Better Each Day

My Challenge

Let Go Of

Tomorrow I Will

HIGHLIGHTS

Date: /   /

Highlights of the Day

1.

2.

3.

What is something new you've learned?

What were some challenges you faced?

What is the best thing you have done for yourself today?

Has practicing gratitude helped you today?

YES   MAYBE   NO

DAILY GRATITUDE JOURNAL

Date: /   /

Today I am grateful for

Quotes & Affirmations

Looking Forward To Today

Things that make me happy

Getting Better Each Day

My Challenge

Let Go Of

Tomorrow I Will

HIGHLIGHTS

Date: /   /

Highlights of the Day

1.

2.

3.

What is something new you've learned?

What were some challenges you faced?

What is the best thing you have done for yourself today?

Has practicing gratitude helped you today?

YES   MAYBE   NO

DAILY GRATITUDE JOURNAL

Date: /   /

Today I am grateful for

Quotes & Affirmations

Looking Forward To Today

Things that make me happy

Getting Better Each Day

My Challenge

Let Go Of

Tomorrow I Will

HIGHLIGHTS

Date: / /

Highlights of the Day

1.

2.

3.

What is something new you've learned?

What were some challenges you faced?

What is the best thing you have done for yourself today?

Has practicing gratitude helped you today?

YES   MAYBE   NO

DAILY GRATITUDE JOURNAL

Date: /   /

Today I am grateful for

Quotes & Affirmations

Looking Forward To Today

Things that make me happy

Getting Better Each Day

My Challenge

Let Go Of

Tomorrow I Will

HIGHLIGHTS

Date: /   /

Highlights of the Day

1.

2.

3.

What is something new you've learned?

What were some challenges you faced?

What is the best thing you have done for yourself today?

Has practicing gratitude helped you today?

YES   MAYBE   NO

DAILY GRATITUDE JOURNAL

Date: /   /

Today I am grateful for

Quotes & Affirmations

Looking Forward To Today

Things that make me happy

Getting Better Each Day

My Challenge

Let Go Of

Tomorrow I Will

HIGHLIGHTS

Date: /   /

Highlights of the Day

1.

2.

3.

What is something new you've learned?

What were some challenges you faced?

What is the best thing you have done for yourself today?

Has practicing gratitude helped you today?

| YES | MAYBE | NO |

DAILY GRATITUDE JOURNAL

Date: /   /

Today I am grateful for

Quotes & Affirmations

Looking Forward To Today

Things that make me happy

Getting Better Each Day

My Challenge

Let Go Of

Tomorrow I Will

HIGHLIGHTS

Date: /   /

Highlights of the Day

1.

2.

3.

What is something new you've learned?

What were some challenges you faced?

What is the best thing you have done for yourself today?

Has practicing gratitude helped you today?

| YES | MAYBE | NO |

DAILY GRATITUDE JOURNAL

Date: /   /

Today I am grateful for

Quotes & Affirmations

Looking Forward To Today

Things that make me happy

Getting Better Each Day

My Challenge	Let Go Of	Tomorrow I Will

HIGHLIGHTS

Date: / /

Highlights of the Day

1.

2.

3.

What is something new you've learned?

What were some challenges you faced?

What is the best thing you have done for yourself today?

Has practicing gratitude helped you today?

YES   MAYBE   NO

DAILY GRATITUDE JOURNAL

Date: / /

Today I am grateful for

Quotes & Affirmations

Looking Forward To Today

Things that make me happy

Getting Better Each Day

My Challenge

Let Go Of

Tomorrow I Will

HIGHLIGHTS

Date: /   /

Highlights of the Day

1.

2.

3.

What is something new you've learned?

What were some challenges you faced?

What is the best thing you have done for yourself today?

Has practicing gratitude helped you today?

| YES | MAYBE | NO |

DAILY GRATITUDE JOURNAL

Date: /   /

Today I am grateful for

Quotes & Affirmations

Looking Forward To Today

Things that make me happy

Getting Better Each Day

My Challenge

Let Go Of

Tomorrow I Will

HIGHLIGHTS

Date: /   /

Highlights of the Day

1.

2.

3.

What is something new you've learned?

What were some challenges you faced?

What is the best thing you have done for yourself today?

Has practicing gratitude helped you today?

YES   MAYBE   NO

DAILY GRATITUDE JOURNAL

Date: / /

Today I am grateful for

Quotes & Affirmations

Looking Forward To Today   Things that make me happy

Getting Better Each Day

My Challenge   Let Go Of   Tomorrow I Will

HIGHLIGHTS

Date: /   /

Highlights of the Day

1.

2.

3.

What is something new you've learned?

What were some challenges you faced?

What is the best thing you have done for yourself today?

Has practicing gratitude helped you today?

YES   MAYBE   NO

DAILY GRATITUDE JOURNAL

Date: /   /

Today I am grateful for

Quotes & Affirmations

Looking Forward To Today

Things that make me happy

Getting Better Each Day

My Challenge

Let Go Of

Tomorrow I Will

HIGHLIGHTS

Date: /   /

Highlights of the Day

1.

2.

3.

What is something new you've learned?

What were some challenges you faced?

What is the best thing you have done for yourself today?

Has practicing gratitude helped you today?

YES   MAYBE   NO

DAILY GRATITUDE JOURNAL

Date: /   /

Today I am grateful for

Quotes & Affirmations

Looking Forward To Today

Things that make me happy

Getting Better Each Day

My Challenge

Let Go Of

Tomorrow I Will

HIGHLIGHTS

Date: /   /

Highlights of the Day

1.

2.

3.

What is something new you've learned?

What were some challenges you faced?

What is the best thing you have done for yourself today?

Has practicing gratitude helped you today?

YES	MAYBE	NO

DAILY GRATITUDE JOURNAL

Date: /   /

Today I am grateful for

Quotes & Affirmations

Looking Forward To Today

Things that make me happy

Getting Better Each Day

My Challenge	Let Go Of	Tomorrow I Will

HIGHLIGHTS

Date: /   /

Highlights of the Day

1.

2.

3.

What is something new you've learned?

What were some challenges you faced?

What is the best thing you have done for yourself today?

Has practicing gratitude helped you today?

YES   MAYBE   NO

DAILY GRATITUDE JOURNAL

Date: /   /

Today I am grateful for

Quotes & Affirmations

Looking Forward To Today

Things that make me happy

Getting Better Each Day

My Challenge

Let Go Of

Tomorrow I Will

HIGHLIGHTS

Date: / /

Highlights of the Day

1.

2.

3.

What is something new you've learned?

What were some challenges you faced?

What is the best thing you have done for yourself today?

Has practicing gratitude helped you today?

YES   MAYBE   NO

DAILY GRATITUDE JOURNAL

Date: /   /

Today I am grateful for

Quotes & Affirmations

Looking Forward To Today

Things that make me happy

Getting Better Each Day

My Challenge

Let Go Of

Tomorrow I Will

HIGHLIGHTS

Highlights of the Day

1.

2.

3.

What is something new you've learned?

What were some challenges you faced?

What is the best thing you have done for yourself today?

Has practicing gratitude helped you today?

YES   MAYBE   NO

DAILY GRATITUDE JOURNAL

Date: /   /

Today I am grateful for

Quotes & Affirmations

Looking Forward To Today

Things that make me happy

Getting Better Each Day

My Challenge

Let Go Of

Tomorrow I Will

HIGHLIGHTS

Date: /   /

Highlights of the Day

1.

2.

3.

What is something new you've learned?

What were some challenges you faced?

What is the best thing you have done for yourself today?

Has practicing gratitude helped you today?

YES   MAYBE   NO

DAILY GRATITUDE JOURNAL

Date: /   /

Today I am grateful for

Quotes & Affirmations

Looking Forward To Today

Things that make me happy

Getting Better Each Day

My Challenge

Let Go Of

Tomorrow I Will

HIGHLIGHTS

Highlights of the Day

1.

2.

3.

What is something new you've learned?

What were some challenges you faced?

What is the best thing you have done for yourself today?

Has practicing gratitude helped you today?

YES   MAYBE   NO

DAILY GRATITUDE JOURNAL

Date: /   /

Today I am grateful for

Quotes & Affirmations

Looking Forward To Today

Things that make me happy

Getting Better Each Day

My Challenge

Let Go Of

Tomorrow I Will

HIGHLIGHTS

Date: / /

Highlights of the Day

1.

2.

3.

What is something new you've learned?

What were some challenges you faced?

What is the best thing you have done for yourself today?

Has practicing gratitude helped you today?

YES   MAYBE   NO

DAILY GRATITUDE JOURNAL

Date: /   /

Today I am grateful for

Quotes & Affirmations

Looking Forward To Today

Things that make me happy

Getting Better Each Day

My Challenge

Let Go Of

Tomorrow I Will

HIGHLIGHTS

Date: /   /

Highlights of the Day

1.

2.

3.

What is something new you've learned?

What were some challenges you faced?

What is the best thing you have done for yourself today?

Has practicing gratitude helped you today?

YES   MAYBE   NO

DAILY GRATITUDE JOURNAL

Date: /   /

Today I am grateful for

Quotes & Affirmations

Looking Forward To Today

Things that make me happy

Getting Better Each Day

My Challenge

Let Go Of

Tomorrow I Will

HIGHLIGHTS

Date: /   /

Highlights of the Day

1.

2.

3.

What is something new you've learned?

What were some challenges you faced?

What is the best thing you have done for yourself today?

Has practicing gratitude helped you today?

YES   MAYBE   NO

DAILY GRATITUDE JOURNAL

Date: /   /

Today I am grateful for

Quotes & Affirmations

Looking Forward To Today

Things that make me happy

Getting Better Each Day

My Challenge

Let Go Of

Tomorrow I Will

HIGHLIGHTS

Date: / /

Highlights of the Day

1.

2.

3.

What is something new you've learned?

What were some challenges you faced?

What is the best thing you have done for yourself today?

Has practicing gratitude helped you today?

YES   MAYBE   NO

DAILY GRATITUDE JOURNAL

Date: /   /

Today I am grateful for

Quotes & Affirmations

Looking Forward To Today

Things that make me happy

Getting Better Each Day

My Challenge

Let Go Of

Tomorrow I Will

HIGHLIGHTS

Date: /   /

Highlights of the Day

1.

2.

3.

What is something new you've learned?

What were some challenges you faced?

What is the best thing you have done for yourself today?

Has practicing gratitude helped you today?

YES   MAYBE   NO

DAILY GRATITUDE JOURNAL

Date: / /

Today I am grateful for

Quotes & Affirmations

Looking Forward To Today

Things that make me happy

Getting Better Each Day

My Challenge

Let Go Of

Tomorrow I Will

HIGHLIGHTS

Date: /   /

Highlights of the Day

1.

2.

3.

What is something new you've learned?

What were some challenges you faced?

What is the best thing you have done for yourself today?

Has practicing gratitude helped you today?

YES   MAYBE   NO